For the sake of a single verse . . .

Ben Shahn

for the sake of
a single verse....
from the Note-
books of Malte
Laurids Brigge
by Rainer
Maria Rilke
......
Lithographs
and Afterword
by Ben Shahn

 Clarkson N. Potter, Inc./Publisher NEW YORK

DISTRIBUTED BY CROWN PUBLISHERS, INC

For the Sake of a Single Verse…

LITHOGRAPHS

For the sake of a single verse . . .

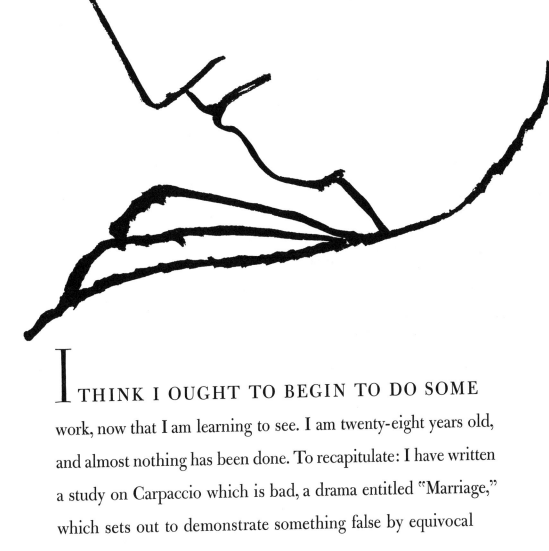

I THINK I OUGHT TO BEGIN TO DO SOME

work, now that I am learning to see. I am twenty-eight years old,

and almost nothing has been done. To recapitulate: I have written

a study on Carpaccio which is bad, a drama entitled "Marriage,"

which sets out to demonstrate something false by equivocal

means, and some verses. Ah! but verses amount to so little when one writes them young. One ought to wait and gather sense and sweetness a whole life long, and a long life if possible, and then, quite at the end, one might perhaps be able to write ten lines that were good. For verses are not, as people imagine, simply feelings (those one has early enough),—they are experiences. For the sake of a single verse, one must see many cities, men and things, one must know the animals, one must feel how the birds fly and know the gesture with which the little flowers open in the morning. One must be able to think back to roads in unknown regions, to unexpected meetings and to partings one had long seen coming; to days of childhood that are still unexplained, to parents whom one had to hurt when they brought one some joy and one did not grasp it (it was a joy for someone else); to childhood illnesses that so strangely begin with such a number of profound and grave transformations, to days in rooms withdrawn and quiet and to mornings by the sea, to the sea itself, to seas, to nights of travel that rushed along on high and flew with all the stars—and it is not yet enough if one may think of all this. One must have memories of many nights of love, none of which was like the others, of the screams of women in labor, and of light, white, sleeping women in childbed, closing again. But one must also have been beside the dying, must have sat beside the dead in the room with the open window and the fitful noises. And still it is not yet enough to have memories. One must be able to forget them when they are many and one must have the great patience to wait until they come again. For it is not yet the memories themselves. Not till they have turned to blood within us, to glance and gesture, nameless and no longer to be distinguished from ourselves—not till then can it happen that in a most rare hour the first word of a verse arises in their midst and goes forth from them.

RAINER MARIA RILKE

I

For the sake of a single verse
one must see many cities,

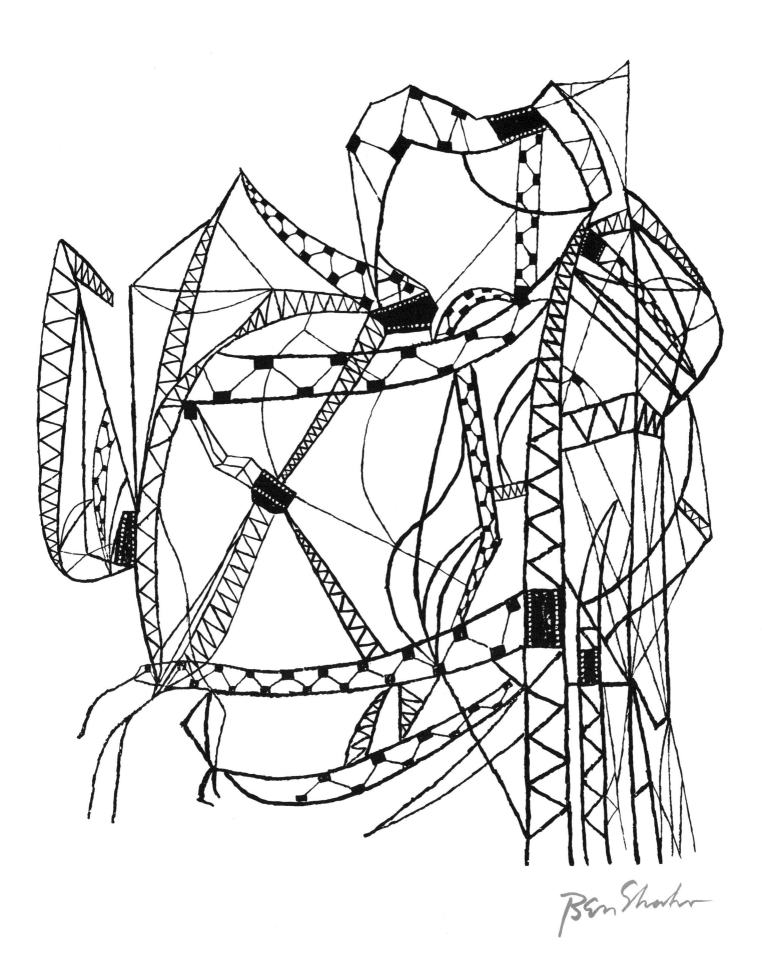

Ben Shahn

II

.... men

III

.... and things,

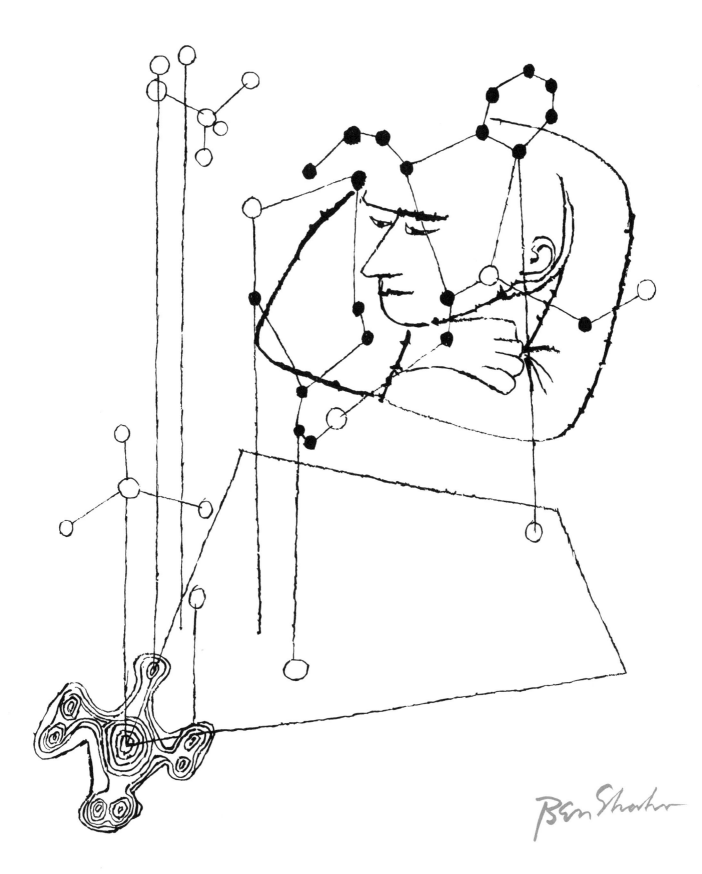

IV

.... one must know the animals,

V

.... one must feel how the birds fly

VI

....and know the gestures with which the little flowers open in the morning.

Ben Shahn

VII

One must be able to think back
to roads in unknown regions,

Ben Shahn

VIII

.... to unexpected meetings

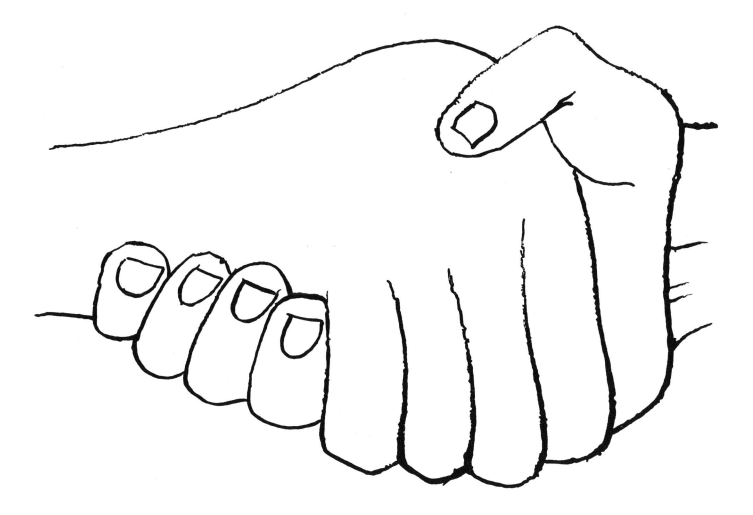

Ben Shahn

IX

....and partings one had long seen coming;

X

.... to days of childhood that are still unexplained,

XI

.... to parents whom
one had to hurt when they brought one
some joy and one did not grasp it
(it was a joy for someone else);

XII

..... to childhood illnesses that so strangely begin with such a number of profound and grave transformations,

XIII

.... to days in rooms withdrawn and quiet

XIV

.... and to mornings by the sea,

XV

....to the sea itself, to seas,

Ben Shahn

XVI

.... to nights of travel that rushed
along on high and flew with
all the stars—

XVII

.... and it is not yet enough if one may think of all this. One must have memories of many nights of love, none of which was like the others,

XVIII

.... of the screams of women in labor

XIX

....and of light, white sleeping
women in childbed, closing again.

XX

But one must also have been
beside the dying,

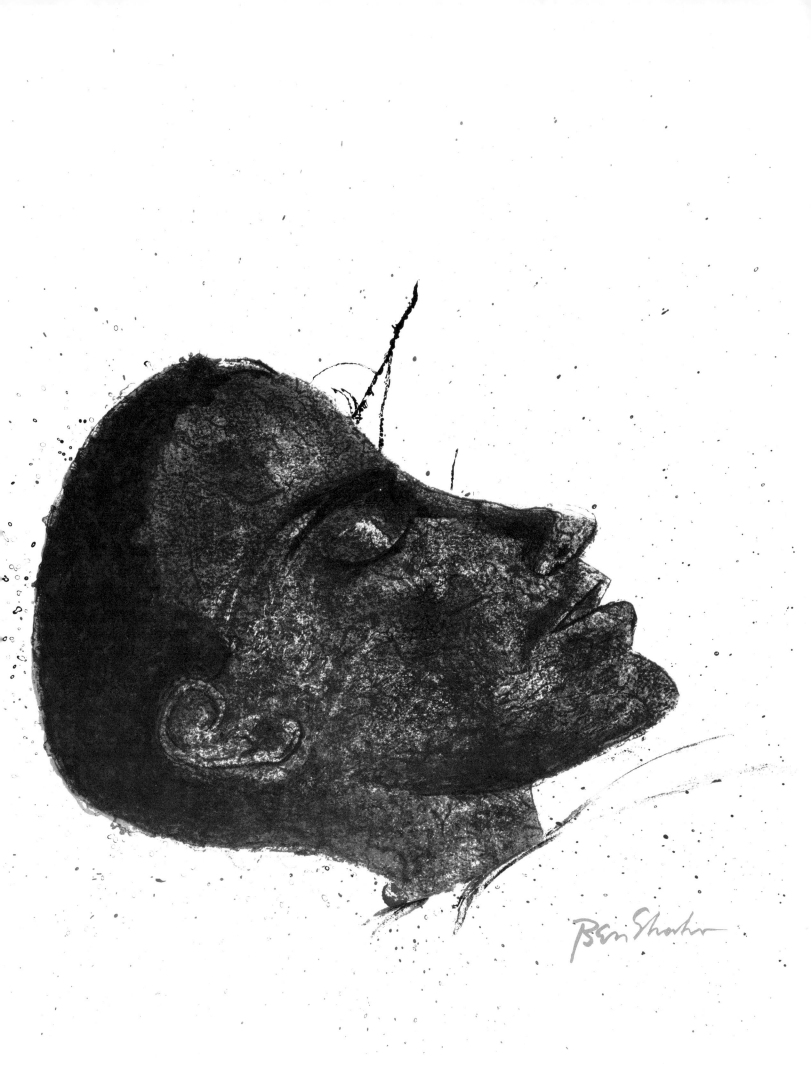

XXI

.... must have sat
beside the dead in the room
with the open window and the
fitful noises.

XXII

One must be able to forget them when
they are many and one must
have the great patience to wait
until they come again. For it is
not yet the memories themselves.
Not till they have turned to blood
within us, to glance and gesture,
nameless and no longer to be
distinguished from ourselves—
not till then can it happen that
in a most rare hour the first
word of a verse arises in their
midst and goes forth from them.

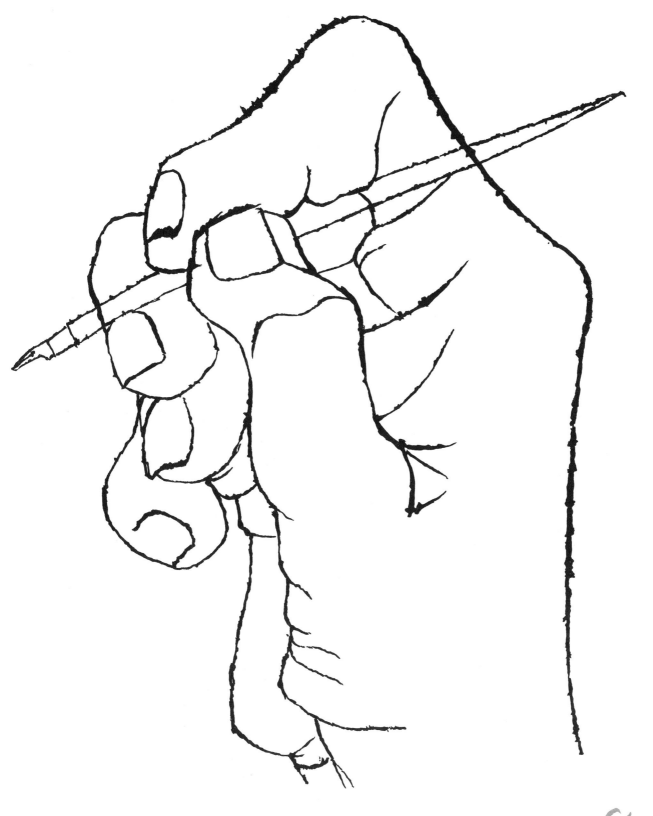

I was twenty-eight years old; I had just recently arrived in Paris. I had certainly never heard of Rainer Maria Rilke when I found on one of the bookstalls along the Seine a small volume called "Les Cahiers de Malte Laurids Brigge." I was entranced by the writer's observations, not just upon Paris, but on life itself. Malte Brigge had only just arrived in Paris when the notebooks began. He too was twenty-eight. This young man seemed almost to be me.

I had arrived in Paris via the Gare de l'Est. I had walked and walked, never getting enough of seeing and being where I was. I came to know Boulevard de Sebastopol, then the networks of little streets, Rue du Roi de Sicile, Rue des Rosiers, Rue des Francs Bourgeois. I made the Carnavalet my personal museum; Place des Vosges was my own private retreat. I was the discoverer; surely no one had seen this place as I now saw it.

I imagined that Rilke had arrived in Paris by way of the Gare d'Austerlitz. He had walked along the Seine, crossed to the Ile de la Cité where he came upon the Hôtel Dieu and made in that vicinity so many touching observations. Such was the beginning of my sense of kinship with Rilke.

But there were other and more profound reasons for this kinship. Like every young artist under the sun, I was intent upon finding the deep and abiding way of things. I read the constantly proliferating art literature of the late Twenties in Paris — the manifestos, the tracts, the declarations, the testaments, the confessions, the diaries, the autobiographies, the monographs, always seeking the clue, the magic key to what was what, the elusive ingredient that made art, art, and not just more paint upon canvas, more filled-up space.

There must be something, I thought — as young artists still think, and that they still seek — some knowledge that must be possessed by the elect, that must endow them with those especial powers not possessed by ordinary persons.

But however avid my reading, my looking, seeking, pondering, I did not find any such clue at all. The tracts and the manifestos said too much the same thing. Oh, certainly, line, form, color, texture were the stuff of the images of art — no denying that. But one had to be honest with himself; this was all rudimentary. Essential, indeed, but there was more. There was something further that infused an image that gave it life. I agreed with the manifesto-writers that art should not be burdened by mission to uplift, nor should it be loaded with academic rules and principles. I was as ready as anyone to throw off the traces and be free.

But I wanted to be free also of the new academy that was already moving in, already setting up its cast-iron rules for the new generation of painters. Indeed it did create them, and indeed the artists of today are still tyrannized over by its grim ethic of disengagement. (When will they free themselves? Who knows?)

Alone now in my thinking, I began to believe that art did, after all, have a mission — certainly not the Beaux-Arts kind of mission, but another one. Its mission was to tell what I felt, to say what I thought, to be my own declaration. I could not accept the current ones; they expressed some other fellow's beliefs and intentions, not mine. Pictures would be my manifesto.

Rilke wrote: "I am learning to see; yes, I am beginning to see." How wonderful! No one could take that away from him. That is the great experience of life. No one would take it away from me either. It is tempting to be part of the avant-garde, it is so exciting to be part of a movement, daring and yet secure. But it is an illusion and it creates within the painter a complaisant sense of having done things which in truth he has not done.

The way to painting is a lonely road, a one-man path. It holds no security; it is not cozy. Every moment of painting is a moment of doubting. The only criterion is the criterion of self, of what one wants, what one thinks he believes, his own shaky philosophy. There are no guideposts, no maps, no geography to tell him that he is on the right path. No friend, however sympathetic he may be, can predict the quality or the validity of the image that the painter hopes to bring forth. The only vindication of his course of action is a realized image, a work of art.

I read and was so lured by the manifestos. I avoided them but still with a great nostalgia to participate in the socializing and the ferment that were a part of them — of what today would be called "the scene." But I knew they were foreign to me and that in truth there was for me no choice.

I had now long ago found in Rilke the passage that came to mean so much to me. Here was a writer about the processes of art who was not telling me what to do, what to think, how to paint. No; he was too engrossed in his own discoveries. He was sharing with me the doubts and the hesitations of art, the probings, the slow emergence of forms. His every line of writing was art, and yet such art was inseparable from its life content. No manifesto could ever tell me more clearly than this one paragraph of Rilke's that art is an emanation from a person; that it is shaped and formed out of the shape and form of that person. In being so acutely personal to him it achieves also a rare universality. Rilke is speaking, (is he not?) to the innermost recesses of the consciousness, an area in which we spend so much of our time and expend so much of our feeling, and yet an area that is so remote from communication with our fellow-beings, an area that is, unhappily, increasingly remote from the reaches of art.

The portfolio containing the original
lithographs by Ben Shahn was
completed in 1968 on the presses of
Atelier Mourlot in New York.

Typography by The Spiral Press.

This first edition in book form
has been printed
for the publishers by
The Meriden Gravure Company.